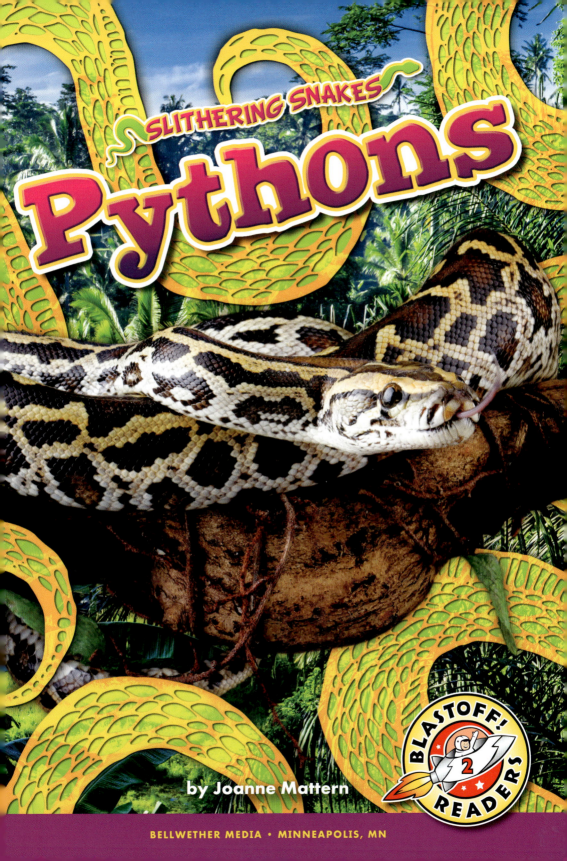

Blastoff! Readers are carefully developed by literacy experts to build reading stamina and move students toward fluency by combining standards-based content with developmentally appropriate text.

Level 1 provides the most support through repetition of high-frequency words, light text, predictable sentence patterns, and strong visual support.

Level 2 offers early readers a bit more challenge through varied sentences, increased text load, and text-supportive special features.

Level 3 advances early-fluent readers toward fluency through increased text load, less reliance on photos, advancing concepts, longer sentences, and more complex special features.

★ **Blastoff! Universe**

This edition first published in 2026 by Bellwether Media, Inc.

No part of this publication may be reproduced in whole or in part without written permission of the publisher. For information regarding permission, write to Bellwether Media, Inc., Attention: Permissions Department, 3500 American Blvd W, Suite 150, Bloomington, MN 55431.

Library of Congress Cataloging-in-Publication Data

LC record for Pythons available at: https://lccn.loc.gov/2025001560

Text copyright © 2026 by Bellwether Media, Inc. BLASTOFF! READERS and associated logos are trademarks and/or registered trademarks of Bellwether Media, Inc. Bellwether Media is a division of FlutterBee Education Group.

Editor: Kieran Downs   Designer: Brittany McIntosh

Printed in the United States of America, North Mankato, MN.

Table of Contents

Large Snakes	4
The Big Squeeze	12
A Python Grows Up	18
Glossary	22
To Learn More	23
Index	24

Large Snakes

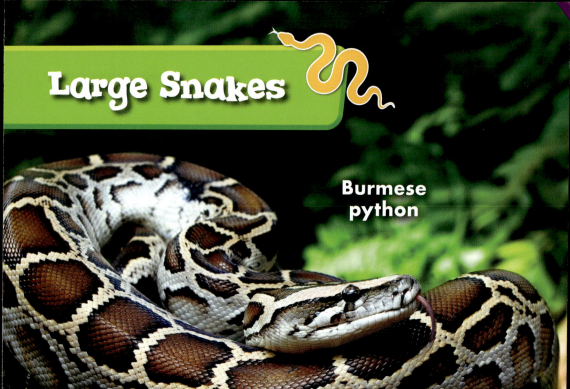

Burmese python

Pythons are large snakes. There are over 40 **species** of pythons.

These **reptiles** like warm, wet places. They are **native** to Asia, Africa, and Australia.

Burmese Python Range

range =

reticulated python

Pythons are the largest snakes in the world. They can be up to 33 feet (10 meters) long!

They can weigh over 300 pounds (136 kilograms).

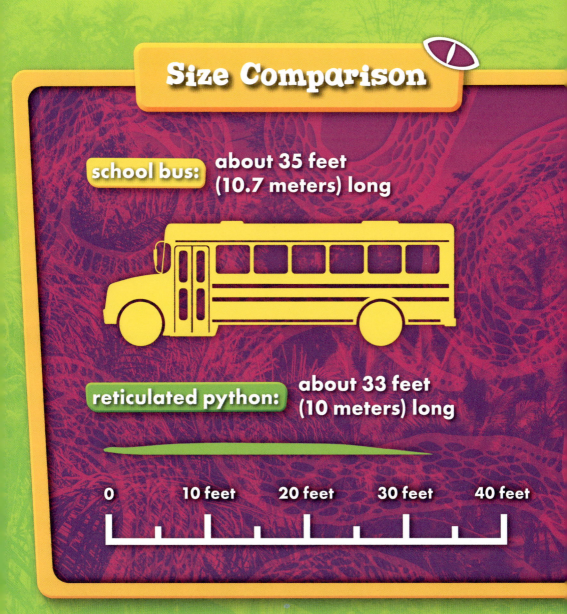

Pythons come in many colors. Some pythons are tan with dark spots. Others are green.

green tree python

A python's color helps it **camouflage** itself.

Pythons have triangle-shaped heads. Some have **pit organs** near their jaws.

The pit organs sense heat. They help pythons find **prey** in the dark.

Spot a Burmese Python!

tan body

dark spots

pit organs

The Big Squeeze

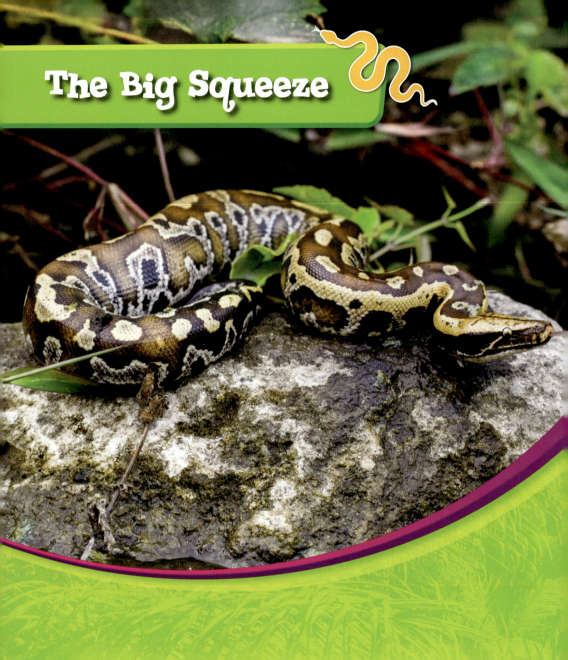

Pythons mostly live in **rain forests** and swamps. They like to hide in tree branches.

They hunt for prey any time of day.

Pythons mostly eat **rodents** and birds. They can eat large prey like wild boars, too.

Pythons are **constrictors**. They squeeze prey until it stops breathing. Their jaws stretch wide to swallow prey whole.

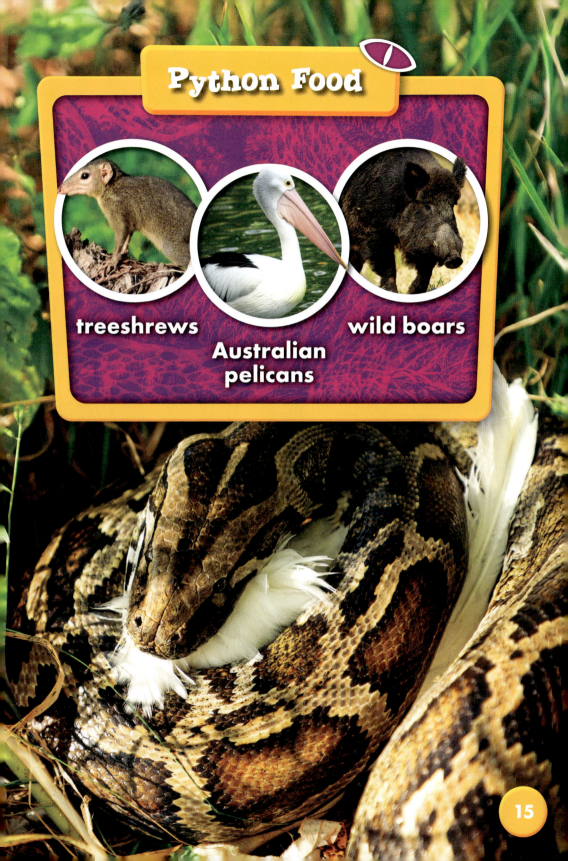

Python Food

treeshrews

Australian pelicans

wild boars

Predators like birds and hyenas eat small pythons. Lions and leopards hunt larger pythons.

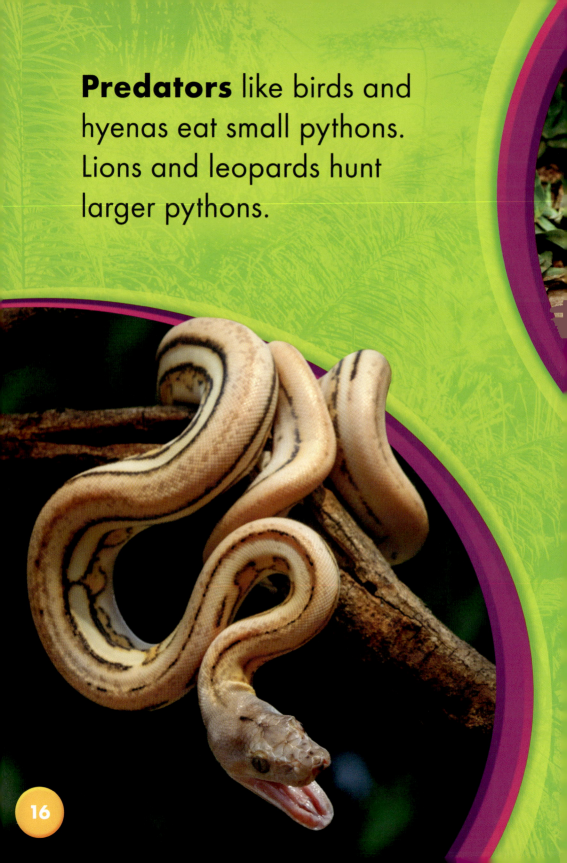

Pythons will strike at predators. Other times they curl into a ball to stay safe.

A Python Grows Up

Pythons lay eggs once per year. They keep the eggs in nests.

Female pythons curl up around the eggs to keep them warm.

Once the babies **hatch** from eggs, they can take care of themselves.

Pythons like to live alone. These snakes are an important part of our world!

hatching

Burmese Python Stats

status in the wild: vulnerable

life span: 20 years

Glossary

camouflage—to use colors and patterns to help an animal hide in its surroundings

constrictors—snakes that squeeze their prey

hatch—to break out of an egg

native—originally from a certain place

pit organs—body parts that help snakes sense heat

predators—animals that hunt other animals for food

prey—animals that are hunted by other animals for food

rain forests—thick, green forests that receive a lot of rain

reptiles—cold-blooded animals that have backbones and lay eggs

rodents—small animals that gnaw on their food

species—kinds of animals

To Learn More

AT THE LIBRARY

Huddleston, Emma. *Burmese Pythons*. Lake Elmo, Minn.: Focus Readers, 2022.

Mattern, Joanne. *Rat Snakes*. Minneapolis, Minn.: Bellwether Media, 2025.

Nguyen, Suzane. *Boa Constrictors*. Minneapolis, Minn.: Bellwether Media, 2025.

ON THE WEB

FACTSURFER

Factsurfer.com gives you a safe, fun way to find more information.

1. Go to www.factsurfer.com.

2. Enter "pythons" into the search box and click 🔍.

3. Select your book cover to see a list of related content.

Index

Africa, 5
alone, 20
Asia, 5
Australia, 5
babies, 20
camouflage, 9
colors, 8, 9, 11
constrictors, 14
eggs, 18, 19, 20
females, 19
food, 14, 15
hatch, 20
heads, 10
hide, 12
hunt, 13, 16
jaws, 10, 14
nests, 18
pit organs, 10, 11
predators, 16, 17
prey, 11, 13, 14
rain forests, 12

range, 5
reptiles, 5
size, 4, 6, 7, 16
species, 4
spots, 8, 11
squeeze, 14
stats, 21
swamps, 12

The images in this book are reproduced through the courtesy of: Agus_Gatam, front cover (snake); Yogdi, front cover (background); Eric Isselee, p. 3; dwi putra stock, p. 4; imageBROKER.com GmbH & Co. KG/ Alamy, p. 6; Kumar Sriskandan/ Alamy, p. 8; Chris Mattison/ Alamy, p. 9; Kurit afshen, pp. 10, 17, 22; asawinimages, p. 11; dwi septiyana, p. 12; Nature Picture Library/ Alamy, p. 13; Wesley Tolhurst, p. 14; Bestkadr, pp. 14-15; Thitiwat. Day, p. 15 (treeshrew); Antoksena, p. 15 (pelican); WildMedia, p. 15 (wild boar); Ralph Padantya, p. 16; Paul Tessier, p. 18; Ken Griffiths, p. 19; Heiko Kiera, p. 20; Girish HC, p. 21.